Rose Rigden's Golf ON THE WILDSIDE

Rose Rigden's

GOLF ON THE WILDSIDE

Published by Footloose Enterprises Ltd
P.O. Box 914, Cambridge, 3450, New Zealand.
www.thenaturalselection.net
footloose@thenaturalselection.co.nz

ISBN 978-0-473-12316-1

Copyright © Footloose Enterprises Ltd
Artist Rose Rigden
Origination by ASAP Productions Limited, Hamilton, New Zealand.

www.asapproductions.co.nz
Printed in China

In ancient times, prehistoric man beat the ground with clubs, uttering spine-chilling cries! Anthropologists call this 'primitive self expression'. Today we find modern man exhibiting this behaviour in a game he calls 'GOLF'!

The Artist

Rose lives with her husband in the city of Mutare, on Zimbabwe's eastern border.
She trained at Durban College in South Africa, and has gained worldwide
recognition and awards through her major public exhibitions of fine art.

With years of experience and her accumulation of Wildside humour,
Rose injects a lighter aspect into this serious challenging game.
She invites you, whatever your handicap, to grab your bag, tee-up and drive
off into some strange situations on the fairways and greens.

So even if you hook, slice or miss altogether....

enjoy your

GOLF ON THE WILDSIDE

Apparently golf originated in Scotland.
Certainly it started with club swinging people....

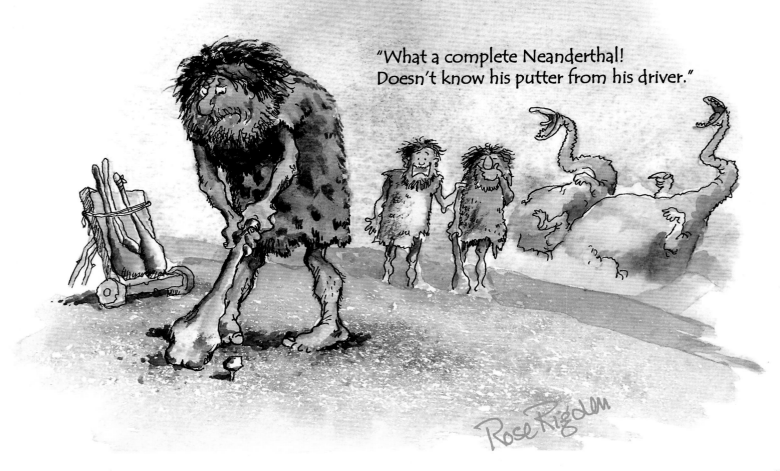

A TOUR OF THE WILDSYDE GOLF COURSE

THE FRONT NINE

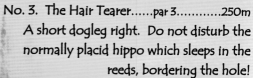

No 1. Outward Bound........par 4.........450m
Several players have complained of being chased
by buffalo and forced to climb trees!
Please choose your tree carefully.

No. 2. The Ripper........par 4............448m
Drive left to avoid a warthog burrow!
Crocodiles in water hazard.
Do not attempt to retrieve balls.

No. 3. The Hair Tearer......par 3............250m
A short dogleg right. Do not disturb the
normally placid hippo which sleeps in the
reeds, bordering the hole!

No. 4. Club Bender...............par 5...............502m
Keep off the tee. A monster trap on the right and
dangerous quicksand along the river bank.
Your caddy should carry a rope.

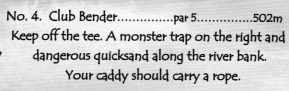

Rose Rigden

8

No. 5. The Snake Park..........par 3..............240m
Concentrate on your putting as there is a
resident black mamba adjacent to the green.

No. 6. The Flapper ....par 4 ...380m

Clear tee shot. Second shot must
cross an elephant trail.
Abandon clubs if charged!

No 7. The Horn......... par 4..........300m
Keep to the right of the fairway.
Everything slopes down to thick bush
where bad tempered black rhino browse.
Be aware of wind direction.

No. 8. Big Loser.........par 5............534m
Keep left to avoid nasty dunes with biting flies!
After a short right dogleg, watch out for ball
stealing meerkats!

No 9. The Killing Grounds.............par 4..........345m
You have to drive straight and long. Bones are strewn over most of
the fairway. Vultures, jackals and hyenas can be a distraction!
Do not dawdle.

Rose Rigden

Rule 11. In the absence of a referee, the players shall refer any dispute to a committee, whose decision shall be final.................

Take time to relax between holes.

Not everyone will celebrate your success.

Rule 26. If a ball lodges in anything moving, the player shall....drop a ball as near as possible to the spot where the object was.........

"These guys are heavy on the carts!"

23

It's good sportsmanship not to pick up golf
balls while they are still rolling.

"Your turn to roar as he swings!"

A bad slice!

Try and play on your opponent's nerves!

Ignore casual advice!

"Skied that one!"

38

Rule 27. ....if a player's ball be stopped...
by an opponent.... the opponent shall lose the hole.........

"We would have been on the green for two if you hadn't hit this guy!"

Some tough courses!

A TOUR OF THE WILDSYDE GOLF COURSE

THE BACK NINE

No. 10. Big Biter.......par 4.....203m

No problems off the tee.
Undulating ground and
scrub provide cover for
resident predators.
Let your caddy retrieve lost balls.

No 11. Plains To See...par 5....490m

A vast expanse with
seasonal wildebeest migrations
causing serious dust and lengthy hold ups.
A GPS is recommended!

No. 12. The Widow Maker...
par 4...340m Take your time
and focus on survival!
Rough ground is home
to the Big Five and
venomous snakes.

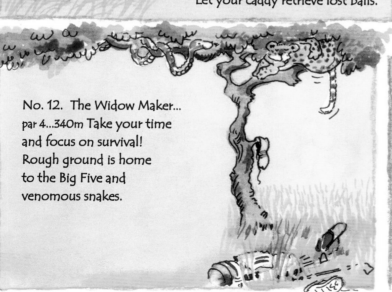

No 13. The Swamp......par 3......230m
This hole really has no fairway!
A three-shotter dogleg right leads
to a treacherous swampy region.
Habitat of the toe sucking toad
and bull-necked red leaches.
Ball retrieval not recommended.

Rose Rigden

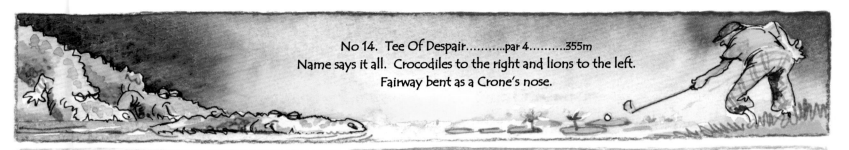

No 14. Tee Of Despair...........par 4..........355m
Name says it all. Crocodiles to the right and lions to the left.
Fairway bent as a Crone's nose.

No. 15. The Hide.........par 4..........340m
Problems from the tee onward. Ball visibility poor. Thorn trees in profusion. Avoid razor grass, stinging buffalo beans and the sap of the spottle wart vine.

No. 16. On the Rocks...........par 5.............480m
It's a boulder and rock strewn fairway.
Carrion eaters perched in stunted trees.
Watch out for ball eating rock rabbits.

No 18. Pride of the Club............par 3....................240m
Classic hole with layered bunkers.
All caddy advice should be whispered.

No. 17. Politicians' Delight.......par 4........380m
From the tee its all crooked and devious!
You want to go left but instinct
dictates 'go right'.
And very few can keep
on the straight.

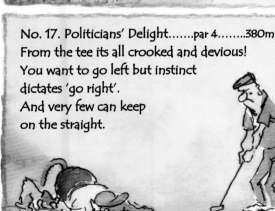

The Pride usually
sleep from 11am to 4pm and
do not like the smell of golfers.
There is a clear escape route marked
together with a refuge pole. Good Luck!

Rose Rigden

49

"Little things please little minds!"

Rule 25. If your ball lands near litter.... remove the litter and replace your ball on its spot........

"Are you sure this is the short cut?"

"Make my day."

Rule 37. ..the player may send his own caddie forward to mark the position of the ball..........

"Well it can't have vanished into thin air!"

That's not a Birdie!

If you drink, don't drive. Don't even putt!

Always choose the right club!

"Let's leave my hips out of this shall we....?"

"I think it would be wise to let him play through."

70

Never play golf with a cheetah.

Rule 31. 'A moveable obstruction may be removed....'

"Looking for something?"

"What baboon designed this course?"

75

Never question your opponent's score on the eighteenth!

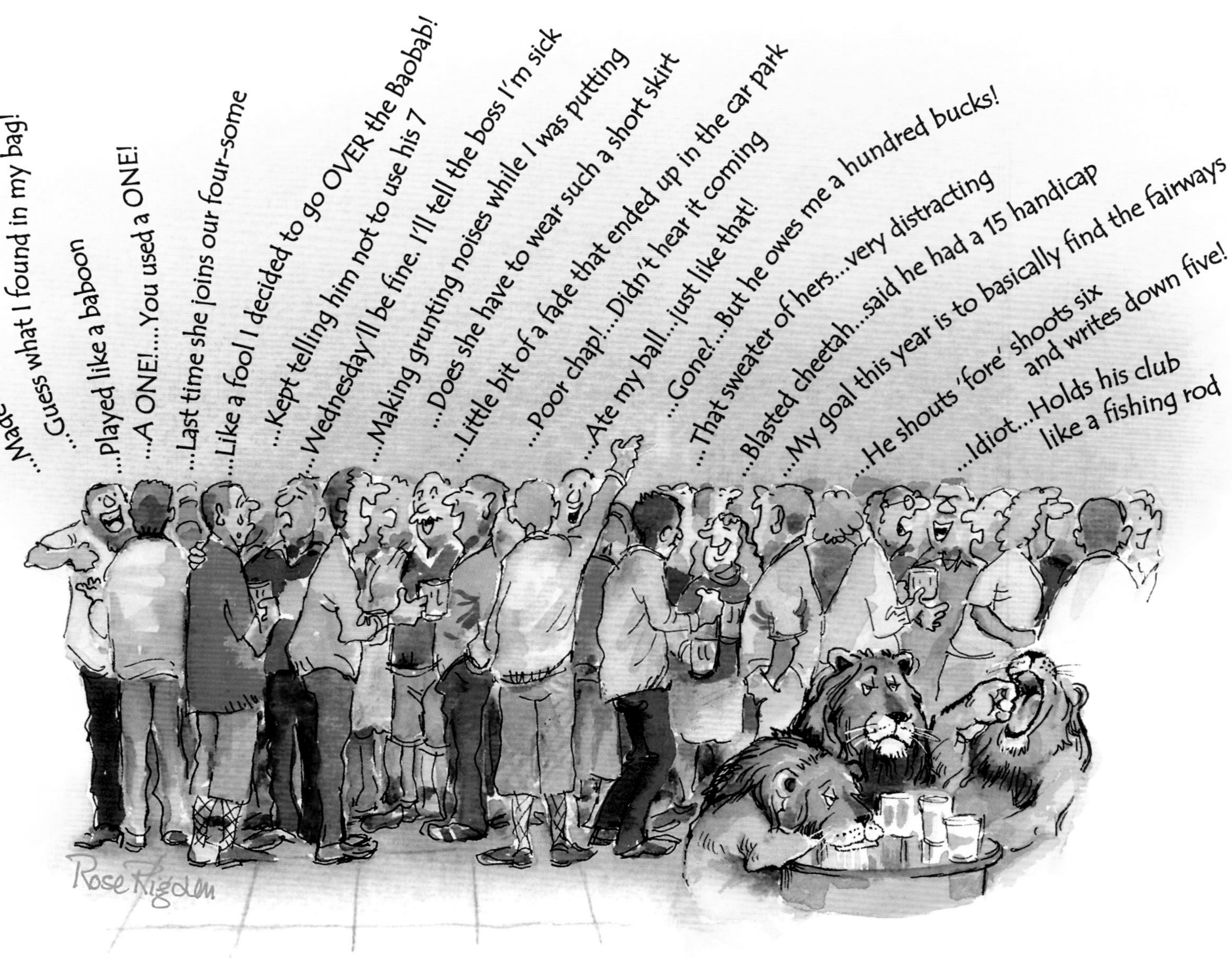
...Made a run for the nearest tree
...Guess what I found in my bag!
...Played like a baboon
...A ONE!....You used a ONE!
...Last time she joins our four-some
...Like a fool I decided to go OVER the Baobab!
...Kept telling him not to use his 7
...Wednesday'll be fine. I'll tell the boss I'm sick
...Making grunting noises while I was putting
...Does she have to wear such a short skirt
...Little bit of a fade that ended up in the car park
...Poor chap!...Didn't hear it coming
...Ate my ball...just like that!
...Gone?...But he owes me a hundred bucks!
...That sweater of hers...very distracting
...Blasted cheetah...said he had a 15 handicap
...My goal this year is to basically find the fairways
...He shouts 'fore' shoots six and writes down five!
...Idiot...Holds his club like a fishing rod
Rose Rigden

Sometimes a golfer makes such a wild shot that when he finally finds the ball, he has lost the course!

"That jackal keeps his bar bills as low as his golf scores!"

"Man! That must be some sand trap."

"Won't you join us for a friendly foursome?"

Rose Rigden

"I hate it when he gets a hole in one."

A challenging day at the club.

Rule 35. The player may move any loose impediment on the green by picking it up....

It's hard to get past the 19th hole!

Rose Rigden

"Don't be such a wimp! It's only a rat."

If a ball of anyone not engaged in the match interferes with play, it may be lifted.....